Discover
ALLIGATORS
&
CROCODILES

by Victoria Marcos

xist Publishing

Alligators have been around for about 37 million years. There are two remaining alligator species - the American alligator and the Chinese alligator.

American alligators weigh around 800 pounds and are about 13 feet long. Chinese alligators are smaller, weighing only around 120 pounds and growing to seven feet long. Their long, flat, muscular tails help them swim.

American alligators live in fresh water such as ponds, lakes, rivers, swamps, and marshes. Chinese alligators are extremely endangered and only a few are left in the wild. They only live in the Yangtze River valley.

7

American alligators live in all of Florida and Louisiana and many parts of the southeastern United States. There are over a million alligators in both Florida and Louisiana

9

Alligators can eat small animals with a single bite. They kill larger prey by pulling it into the water and drowning it. They also roll around with their prey in the water to tear off bite-size chunks they can easily eat.

Large male alligators are solitary and territorial although smaller males gather in groups. Alligators are shy around humans and will usually walk or swim away if someone approaches.

Alligators and crocodiles look very similar and are sometimes difficult to tell apart.

Alligators have shorter heads, more "U-shaped" snouts, and only their top teeth are visible when their mouths are closed.

Crocodiles have longer heads and more "V-shaped" snouts. If you look at them from the side when their mouths are shut, most of their teeth are visible.

Crocodiles are also much more aggressive than alligators.

Crocodiles vary in size significantly. The dwarf crocodile grows to only about 6 feet long and weighs no more than 70 pounds while the saltwater crocodile can grow to 23 feet long and weigh up to 2,200 pounds.

19

Crocodiles are very social. They spend a lot of time feeding and basking together. Crocodiles are also very vocal. They gave different calls for different reasons.

Crocodiles are ambush predators. They wait for their prey to come near them, and then they attack. Crocodiles eat mostly fish, birds, amphibians, reptiles and mammals. They are cold-blooded reptiles with a very slow metabolism which means they can go long periods without food.

23

Crocodiles have excellent senses. Their nose, eyes and ears are on the top of their heads allowing them to be almost entirely underwater and hidden from their prey.

Crocodiles have webbing on the toes of their hind feet that helps them make quick turns in the water. The webbing also helps them swim fast when the first enter the water.

Crocodiles have hard skin that protects them like armor does. Their bellies and sides are smooth. Although their hard skin is thick they are still able to absorb heat from the sun.

29

Both alligators and crocodiles lay eggs. When the eggs hatch, the babies use their "egg-tooth" on the tip of their snouts to help them get out of their egg. Their mother hears their cries and takes them in her mouth one at a time to the water.

Newly hatched alligators stay with their mothers for about two years. Then they are on their own.
Alligators and crocodiles are dangerous predators.